Facilitator's Guide

The

Student

Evaluation

Standards

Lori A. Wingate
The Evaluation Center, Western Michigan University
for The Joint Committee on Standards
for Educational Evaluation
Arlen R. Gullickson, Chair

A Joint Publication of

CORWIN PRESS
A Sage Publications Company
Thousand Oaks, California

ETS *EDUCATIONAL
POLICY LEADERSHIP
INSTITUTE*

For information:

Corwin Press
A Sage Publications Company
2455 Teller Road
Thousand Oaks, California 91320
www.corwinpress.com

Sage Publications Ltd.
6 Bonhill Street
London EC2A 4PU
United Kingdom

Sage Publications India Pvt. Ltd.
B-42, Panchsheel Enclave
Post Box 4109
New Delhi 110 017 India

Printed in the United States of America

Library of Congress Cataloging-in-Publication Data

Wingate, Lori A.
Facilitator's guide to the student evaluation standards / by Lori A. Wingate.
    p. cm.
At head of title: Joint Committee on Standards for Educational Evaluation.
Includes bibliographical references.
ISBN 0-7619-3131-7 (Paper)
    1. Educational tests and measurements—Standards—United States—Handbooks, manuals, etc. 2. Students—Rating of—United States—Handbooks, manuals, etc.
I. Joint Committee on Standards for Educational Evaluation. II. Title.
LB3051.W49974 2004
371.26--dc21

                                        2003012380

This book is printed on acid-free paper.

03 04 05 06 07 10 9 8 7 6 5 4 3 2 1

Acquisitions Editor:	Faye Zucker
Editorial Assistant:	Stacy Wagner
Production Editor:	Julia Parnell
Proofreader:	Teresa Herlinger
Cover Designer:	Michael Dubowe
Typesetting:	Lori Wingate

Contents

Acknowledgments

I wish to extend my gratitude to Arlen Gullickson, Chair of the Joint Committee on Standards for Educational Evaluation, who gave me the assignment to develop this guide and provided valuable guidance and support. I am indebted to Paula Egelson and Barbara Howard at SERVE, who generously shared their expertise and experience with me. I also received excellent advice from Barbara Bichelmeyer from Indiana University. Joint Committee members Patty McDivitt, Todd Rogers, and Donald Yarbrough provided valuable feedback on the guide in its various stages of development, as did Amy Gullickson. From The Evaluation Center, I also thank Dale Farland and Sally Veeder for their careful review and suggestions. Donna Bearden from Dallas Independent School District graciously allowed me to use a program she developed with JoAnne Hughes and other district staff as the basis for one of the case examples. I am grateful to Anne Smith and Flo Frank, whose publication—*The Community Development Facilitator's Guide: A Tool to Support the Community Development Handbook*, developed for Human Resources Development Canada—I used as a model for this guide. I also thank Faye Zucker from Corwin Press for her helpful support throughout the development of the guide. As the author, however, I take full responsibility for any limitations or deficiencies in the guide.

Lori A. Wingate

About the Authors

The Joint Committee on Standards for Educational Evaluation

Chair

Arlen Gullickson (1998 – present)
James R. Sanders (1988 – 1998)

Vice Chair

Arlen Gullickson (1995 – 1998)
Jerry Horn (1998 – 2002)

Committee Members

Edith Beatty, representing the Association for Supervision and Curriculum Development (ASCD)

Rolf Blank, representing the Council of Chief State School Officers (CCSSO)

Fred Brown, representing the National Association of Elementary School Principals (NAESP)

Flora Caruthers, representing the National Legislative Program Evaluation Society (NLPES)

Jim Cullen, representing the Canadian Evaluation Society (CES)

Glen Cutlip, representing the National Education Association (NEA)

Paula Egelson and Todd Rogers, representing the Consortium for Research on Educational Accountability and Teacher Evaluation (CREATE)

Patricia McDivitt, representing the American Counseling Association (ACA)

Jack Naglieri, representing the American Psychological Association (APA)

Dianna Newman, representing the American Evaluation Association (AEA)

Michael Resnick, representing the National School Boards Association (NSBA)

Lyn Shulha, representing the Canadian Society for the Study of Education (CSSE)

Gary Wegenke, representing the American Association of School Administrators (AASA)

Mark Wilson, representing the American Educational Research Association (AERA)

Donald Yarbrough, representing the National Council on Measurement in Education (NCME)

Arlen R. Gullickson, Ph.D., is Director of The Evaluation Center and Professor of Education at Western Michigan University, Kalamazoo, Michigan. Since 1998, he has served as chair of the Joint Committee on Standards for Educational Evaluation. His and the Center's work focuses on improving the theory and practice of evaluation. His writing includes books, chapters, and articles on evaluation. Much of his writing has focused on teacher preparation and practices for evaluation of students and on improving teachers' assessment practices. He directs an annual national institute on evaluation and provides extensive support for evaluation through the Center's Web site at http://evaluation.wmich.edu.

Lori A. Wingate, M.A., is Assistant to the Director of The Evaluation Center at Western Michigan University, Kalamazoo, Michigan. She began her career in evaluation by coordinating a judicial performance evaluation program. During her tenure at The Evaluation Center, she has evaluated programs in diverse areas, including community and housing development, science literacy, technology literacy, and transportation. She is editor and manager of the Evaluation Checklists Web site (http://evaluation.wmich.edu/checklists) and assistant editor of the *International Handbook of Educational Evaluation.*

Facilitator Information

About the Guide

This facilitator's guide is intended to be a supplement to *The Student Evaluation Standards: How to Judge Evaluations of Students*, by The Joint Committee on Standards for Educational Evaluation, Arlen R. Gullickson, Chair, Thousand Oaks, CA, Corwin Press, 2003 (www.corwinpress.com). *The Student Evaluation Standards* provide guidance for assessing and improving student evaluation practices and policies. The 28 standards are organized around the attributes of propriety, utility, feasibility, and accuracy.

This guide provides a framework for introducing educators and other education stakeholders to *The Student Evaluation Standards*. It presents a series of lesson plans for workshop activities to support the general understanding and application of the Standards and promote sound student evaluation practices and policies.

This first section of the guide, "Facilitator Information," provides information about the workshop objectives, potential participants, logistics, materials, design, and the facilitator's role. This section also includes some frequently asked questions to aid facilitators in answering questions about the Standards. The "Workshop Activities" section presents a series of lesson plans for workshop activities, grouped in three parts: Orientation, Introduction to *The Student Evaluation Standards*, and Conclusion. The final section, "Workshop Materials," includes handouts and overheads, which may be photocopied for use in the workshops.

To use this guide effectively for planning and conducting workshops on the Standards, it is very important that facilitators read and become familiar with the contents of *The Student Evaluation Standards*.

Workshop Objectives

The overarching goal of the Student Evaluation Standards workshop presented in this guide is to make participants aware of the Standards and their importance in supporting student learning. In support of this goal, the workshop objectives are for participants to

- develop a common understanding of the nature of student evaluation, including the range of activities and purposes associated with student evaluation
- become acquainted with the contents and organization of *The Student Evaluation Standards*
- apply the Standards in order to understand their relevance and applicability
- identify ways to use the Standards (as teachers, administrators, parents/guardians, university instructors, and others who evaluate students and/or have a legitimate need for student evaluation results)

Workshop Participants

Workshop organizers and facilitators are encouraged to think broadly in terms of potential workshop participants. Student evaluation plays a central role in education, and there are many important stakeholders—persons involved in and/or affected by student evaluations. These include, but are not limited to

- teachers
- guidance counselors
- school psychologists
- curriculum directors
- principals
- superintendents
- school improvement team members
- school board members
- community members
- parents/guardians
- college/university instructors involved in teacher preparation
- students

Although students are most immediately affected by student evaluations, this guide was not developed with student workshop participants in mind. However, for workshops with diverse roles represented, workshop organizers may find value in including some high school students.

Workshop Logistics

The facilitator is responsible for making sure the workshop environment is conducive to learning and participation by all workshop attendees. Logistical considerations should be attended to well in advance, so that valuable workshop time is not used for locating/fixing equipment, rearranging seating, or participants going in search of refreshments, etc.

The ideal number of workshop participants is 12–20. It is preferable to arrange seating in the room to promote discussion (e.g., U-shape, circle, or round table). Participants should have enough room to move their chairs around or move to other seating areas in the room in order to work in small groups.

Workshop Materials

A copy of *The Student Evaluation Standards* should be provided to all workshop participants at least one week in advance of the workshop. Participants should be encouraged to read as much of the book as possible before the workshop. At a minimum, each participant should read the book's introduction and one complete standard in preparation for the workshop. A sample letter to include when the book is provided to participants in advance of a workshop is provided in Appendix A.

In planning for the workshop, identify what equipment or supplies will be needed. These include the following items:
- name tags
- flip chart(s)
- flip chart paper (blank and prepared)

- overhead projector or computer projector
- masking tape
- colored markers
- index cards
- 3" x 5" sticky notes (e.g., Post-It® notes)
- bowl or other container (see Activity 2.4)
- overheads
  - Definition of Student Evaluation (Appendix C)
  - Standards Summaries (Appendices D1-D4)
- handouts (1 copy per participant except where noted)
  - Agenda (sample provided in Appendix B)
  - Case Example 1: Plagiarism Controversy (Appendix E)
  - Case Example 1 Questions (Appendix F)
  - Standard Application Worksheet (Appendix G)—two copies per small group
  - Case Example 2: Math Learning Communities (Appendix H)
  - Treasure Hunt Questions (Appendix I)—only one copy required
  - Pair-Share Questions (Appendix J)
  - Workshop Evaluation Form (Appendix K)

You may wish to consult the matrix in the next section to determine what materials are required for each activity. Make sure these materials are in place and are operational before the start of the workshop. To save time in distributing materials, you might consider creating packets for participants that include all the handouts (except the Treasure Hunt questions, which are cut up and distributed on separate strips of papers) to be distributed at the beginning of the workshop.

Workshop Design

The activities presented in this guide consist mostly of small-group discussions. Small-group discussion, followed by reporting to the larger group, is an effective way to engage participants and promote analysis and reflection on the topics presented. Small groups should consist of 3 to 5 participants.

It is a good idea to group participants according to number, rather than forming groups based on where they are sitting—because participants who already know each other will tend to sit together. Go around the room and assign each participant a number by counting 1 to 4 (or less, depending on how many groups you want to create). Then group all the 1s together, all the 2s, and so on. It may be beneficial to create new groups for some of the exercises, so that participants can benefit from interacting with a range of other people.

Instructional time for the workshop, as presented in this guide, is approximately 5 hours. Ideally, it would be offered as a 1-day workshop (rather than broken up over multiple days). The matrix below is provided to assist you in preparing for and organizing your workshop.

Activity	Purpose	Materials	Length
1.1 Introductions & Ground Rules	Have everyone introduce themselves; establish ground rules	• name tags • index cards	20 minutes
1.2 Student Evaluation Perceptions & Expectations	Explore preconceived ideas about student evaluation	• flip chart paper (blank and prepared) • colored markers • tape	30 minutes
1.3 Workshop Objectives & Expectations	Establish objectives for the workshop	• agenda (see Appendix B)	15 minutes
1.4 Nature of Student Evaluation	Present a unified definition of student evaluation and orient participants to the importance of student evaluation	• student evaluation definition overhead (Appendix C) • flip chart paper (prepared) • colored markers • tape • sticky notes	45 minutes
2.1 Overview of the Standards	Introduce participants to the Standards	• Standards overheads (Appendices D1-D4)	20 minutes
2.2 Importance and Relevance of Standards	Orient participants to the need for standards	• Case Example 1 (Appendix E) • Case Example 1 questions (Appendix F)	30 minutes
2.3 Applying the Standards	Engage participants in applying the Standards	• Case Example 1 (Appendix E) • Standards Application worksheet (Appendix G) • Case Example 2 (Appendix H) • flip chart paper	1 hour, 15 minutes
2.4 Treasure Hunt	Explore and become familiar with the content and organization of the book	• Treasure Hunt questions (Appendix I) • Sticky notes • container	20 minutes
3.1 Pair-Share Discussion	Reflect on and discuss material presented; identify actions to be taken	• Pair-Share questions (Appendix J)	20 minutes
3.2 Review	Review workshop objectives and expectations	None (large-group discussion)	15 minutes
3.3 Workshop Evaluation	Get evaluative feedback on workshop	• Workshop Evaluation forms (Appendix K)	10 minutes

Even in the most carefully planned workshops, facilitators may experience unexpected situations that threaten to derail the agenda. It is important to try to stay on schedule, but if this proves impossible, facilitators should adjust the schedule midstream, skipping or shortening some activities if necessary. Certain activities are more critical to achieving the workshop objectives than others; if time runs short, every effort should be made to thoroughly complete activities 1.4, 2.1, 2.3 (at least one of the cases), and 3.1.

The Facilitator's Role

The facilitator's role is primarily to provide a structure for learning about the Standards, keep the process on track, facilitate discussion, and answer questions. The facilitator should *not* make decisions for participants, dominate discussions, or criticize participants' ideas.

The following tips should help facilitators fulfill this role:
- Keep an eye on the schedule, noting when each activity starts, and try to wrap it up on time. If you don't know when you started an activity, it will be hard to judge when the allotted time has passed.
- Encourage input from all participants. If some participants seem reluctant to contribute, call on them by name and invite their input. If someone is dominating the discussion, encourage more input from others, rather than discouraging or criticizing the dominant talker.
- Ask open-ended questions such as, *What does the rest of the group think?* and *How did you reach that conclusion?*
- Check understanding—make sure participants understand you and vice versa.
- Role model how you want participants to behave (e.g., don't interrupt, acknowledge all input, listen actively, ask questions, etc.).

Frequently Asked Questions

The following questions and answers are presented to help facilitators anticipate and prepare for participants' questions.

Who developed the Standards?

The Standards were developed by the Joint Committee on Standards for Educational Evaluation. The Joint Committee is composed of representatives from the following organizations:

- American Association of School Administrators
- American Counseling Association
- American Educational Research Association
- American Evaluation Association
- American Psychological Association
- Association for Supervision and Curriculum Development
- Canadian Evaluation Society
- Canadian Society for the Study of Education
- Consortium for Research on Educational Accountability & Teacher Evaluation
- Council of Chief State School Officers
- National Association of Elementary School Principals

- National Council on Measurement in Education
- National Education Association
- National Legislative Program Evaluation Society
- National School Boards Association

In addition, hundreds of volunteers helped to draft, review, and field-test the Standards.

The Joint Committee has published two other sets of evaluation standards: *The Program Evaluation Standards* (1981, 1994) and *The Personnel Evaluation Standards* (1988).

The Standards are certified by the American National Standards Institute as an American National Standard.

There is additional information on the Joint Committee and the development of *The Student Evaluation Standards* in the book's preface.

Am I expected to fully meet all the Standards in all that I do when evaluating students?

No. In fact, in some instances you will find that completely fulfilling one standard or set of standards makes it difficult to meet other standards. For example, creating assessments that are more reliable is often addressed by making the assessment longer. In turn, making the assessment longer complicates such matters as assessment time and feasibility of using the assessment. As the Joint Committee (1994) states in *The Program Evaluation Standards*, "The relative importance of individual standards will differ from situation to situation" (p. 9). Determining which standards absolutely must be met and which are less important should be based on your informed judgment and knowledge of the particular situation.

Should I immediately try to review all my evaluation policies/practices to ensure that they meet the Standards?

Like with most things, a moderate approach to change is recommended. Take on one course, part of a course, policy, or part of a policy (one that you believe is most important to improve); carefully review it against the Standards, and note concrete ways to improve it. Make those changes and monitor the effects to determine if making those changes does improve the teaching-learning situation. Once you are satisfied with your results, then tackle another area.

Should I inform students about the Student Evaluation Standards?

You are encouraged to inform both students and their parents about these standards. Talk to them about the importance of sound student evaluation practices to serve student learning. Engage them in working with you to monitor and improve student evaluation practices and policies. Research on evaluation practices shows that engaging students in such efforts does serve student learning.

Can the Standards be used for standardized testing?

The Student Evaluation Standards are pertinent to many of the issues one encounters in the use of standardized tests. Persons interested in constructing and validating standardized tests would be better served by the *Standards for Educational and Psychological Testing* (American Educational Research Association, American Psychological Association, & National Council on Measurement, 1999). Those standards were specifically developed to guide the development and use of standardized tests. It would be highly appropriate, however, to use *The Student Evaluation Standards* to help teachers plan and prepare students for annual standardized test programs and integrate the results from standardized tests into the classroom learning situation.

Why haven't I heard of the Standards before?

The Student Evaluation Standards was published in early 2003. The organizations that sponsor the Joint Committee have worked to publicize the new Standards to their members. Information about the Standards has been provided at several regional and national meetings. It takes time to reach everyone. The most important and effective avenue for disseminating information about the Standards is through parents, teachers, and administrators who recognize their importance. This workshop is a starting point—do what you can to spread the word!

Workshop Activities

This section presents a series of activity lesson plans to guide workshop planning and facilitation.

1. Orientation

The orientation activities lay the foundation for the workshop and are designed so that participants can meet one another, share perceptions of student evaluation, identify and discuss the workshop objectives, and develop a common understanding of the nature of student evaluation.

Activity 1.1: Introductions and Ground Rules

Time: 20 minutes

Objective: To have everyone (facilitator and participants) introduce themselves and establish the workshop's ground rules.

Advance Preparation: None

Activity:

1. Introduce yourself to the workshop participants. Highlight your interest in student evaluation.

2. Ask the participants to
   - introduce themselves to the group, giving at least their name and role (parent/guardian, teacher, school board member, etc.)
   - indicate the reason they are attending this workshop

3. Describe your role as facilitator, which is, generally, to
   - provide a structure for learning about the Standards
   - keep the process on track
   - facilitate discussion
   - answer questions

4. Establish the ground rules for the workshop. These items should be included:
   - everyone contributes
   - only one person speaks at a time (no interruptions)
   - no one criticizes the opinions of others
   - cell phones are turned off
   - everyone returns promptly from breaks
   - workshop ends on time

5. Distribute a few index cards to each participant.   Tell participants if they think of a "burning question" during the course of the workshop that doesn't seem pertinent to the topic being covered, they should write it on an index card and turn it in to you. You may then address the questions at appropriate times throughout the workshop and/or refer participants to other resources that may answer the questions. Make sure participants know it is OK to ask clarification questions whenever necessary.

Activity 1.2: Student Evaluation Perceptions and Expectations

Time: 30 minutes

Objective: To explore preconceived ideas about student evaluation and have participants view the topic from a variety of perspectives. In a non-threatening, often humorous way, participants bring out their biases within the safety of a small group, which are then shared with the larger group. This allows the facilitator to be aware of any underlying issues that may affect how participants receive the workshop materials. This activity also serves as an icebreaker.

Advance Preparation: Prepare sheets of flip chart paper—use the following examples or create your own stems. Be sure to leave ample space for additional writing. There should be at least as many sheets as small groups.

Student evaluation is like the color _____.	*Student evaluation is like the food _____.*	*Student evaluation is like the toy _____.*	*Student evaluation is like the animal _____.*
Students expect student evaluation to be _____.	*Teachers expect student evaluation to be _____.*	*Administrators expect student evaluation to be _____.*	*Parents/guardians expect student evaluation to be _____.*

Activity:

1. Tape the prepared sheets on the wall. Divide participants into small groups of 3 to 5 people. Give each group a marker of a different color.

2. Tell participants
   - They have 1 minute per sheet to reach consensus and write down their answer.
   - You will let them know when 1 minute has passed and that it is time to move to the next sheet.
   - Each person should take a turn writing his or her group's answer.
   - They should take their seats when they get back to the sheet they started with.

3. Watch the clock and tell the groups when to move to the next sheet.

4. Scan the sheets for interesting/unexpected/unusual comments. Highlight these for discussion, asking the group responsible to elaborate on its response. Encourage questions/comments from the other participants.

Activity 1.3: Workshop Objectives and Expectations

Time: 15 minutes

Objective: To establish the objectives and agenda for the workshop.

Advance Preparation: Prepare a workshop agenda, including the workshop objectives and schedule, and make copies for distribution to participants. A sample agenda is provided in Appendix B.

Activity:

1. Distribute the agenda for the workshop.

2. Point out that *The Student Evaluation Standards* are **not**
   * *curriculum content standards*
   * *standards for student performance*
   * *standards for state/national achievement tests*
   * *standards for professional organizations*
   Rather,
   * *The Student Evaluation Standards are principles and guidelines for assessing and improving student evaluation* **practices and policies within classrooms and schools***.*

3. Review the workshop objectives, which are to
   * develop a common understanding of the nature of student evaluation, including the range of activities and purposes associated with student evaluation
   * become acquainted with the contents and organization of *The Student Evaluation Standards*
   * apply the Standards in order to understand their relevance and applicability
   * identify ways to use the Standards (as teachers, administrators, parents/guardians, university instructors, and others who evaluate students and/or have a legitimate need for student evaluation results)

   You may wish to write these objectives on flip chart paper and post them on a wall.

4. Invite feedback on the workshop's objectives—ask participants if they have any other expectations for the workshop. Record their additional expectations on flip chart paper and tape to a wall (you will refer to both the set objectives and additional expectations at the end of the workshop).

5. Review the schedule.

Activity 1.4: The Nature of Student Evaluation

Time: 45 minutes

Objective: To provide a unified definition of student evaluation and orient participants to the importance of student evaluation.

Advance Preparation: Prepare an overhead of the Definition of Student Evaluation (Appendix C) or write the definition on flip chart paper. Prepare sheets of flip chart paper as follows (leaving ample space for additional writing):

Why does student evaluation matter to students?	*Why does student evaluation matter to teachers?*	*Why does student evaluation matter to administrators?*	*Why does student evaluation matter to parents?*
• *My grades will determine whether I can graduate.*	• *It tells me whether my students are grasping the material being taught.*	• *I depend on teachers' evaluations of students to make decisions about grade promotion.*	• *I need to know how my child is performing in school.*

Activity:

1. Present the Definition of Student Evaluation overhead and read the definition:
    - *Student evaluation is the process of systematically collecting and interpreting information that can be used (1) to inform students and their parents/guardians about the progress they are making toward attaining the knowledge, skills, attitudes, and behaviors to be learned or acquired; and (2) to inform the various personnel who make educational decisions (instructional, diagnostic, placement, promotion, graduation) about students.*

    Note that this is the definition provided in the *Standards*. Make sure everyone understands this definition and has a chance to discuss any needs for clarification. Note the three main actions conveyed in the definition: collecting, interpreting, and informing.

2. Discuss the difference between assessment and evaluation, terms that are sometimes used interchangeably.
    - *Assessment is the process of collecting information about a student (for example, through quizzes, tests, observation, portfolios, performance assessments, etc.)*
    - *Evaluation includes assessment, along with using that information to determine students' strengths, weaknesses, and progress in meeting learning objectives.*
    - *Assessment is necessary, but not sufficient for evaluation.*

3. Divide the participants into small groups. Assign each group a role: student, teacher, administrator, parent/guardian.

4. Ask participants: *Why does student evaluation matter to students/teachers/administrators/ parents?* Tell each group to answer the question from the perspective of their assigned roles. Post the prepared sheets on the wall and have the participants record their answers there.

5. After a 5-minute recording period, have each group walk around to read the other groups' answers. Invite participants to write their comments/questions about the other groups' answers on sticky notes to attach to the flip chart paper. Remind them to check the sticky notes on their own sheets as well before they sit down.

6. Debrief this portion of the activity by inviting comments from the large group at the conclusion of the activity. This time can be restricted to fit your schedule.

7. Ask participants, given what they determined about "why student evaluation matters," to generate a list of **purposes of student evaluation.** Do this as a group, referring to the groups' written statements. Record the purposes on flip chart paper. The list should include such things as
   - identifying content and skills that students have mastered and where they have deficiencies
   - planning future instruction
   - placing students in remedial or advanced classes
   - advising students on what courses to take
   - making decisions about advancement to the next grade level
   - advising students on career planning
   - making determinations about admittance to higher education institutions
   - responding with evaluative feedback to students' in-class responses and behaviors

8. Working from the purposes list (which should remain visible), have the group generate a list of **student evaluation activities.** It may help to prompt discussion by asking, *What happens before and after student evaluation information is collected?* The list should include such things as
   - assessment (quizzes, tests, writing assignments, portfolios, performance assessments, etc.)
   - planning evaluations
   - interpreting assessment results
   - grading
   - reporting evaluation information
   - developing and communicating evaluation policies

9. Note the variety of activities and purposes listed. The following points should be highlighted:
   - *Evaluating students involves more than just testing and grading.*
   - *Student evaluation requires consistent, daily attention to effectively gather, analyze, and use evaluation information to guide student learning.*
   - *Student evaluation can serve many purposes, but the focus should always be on student learning.*

2. Introduction to *The Student Evaluation Standards*

The activities in this section are intended to introduce participants to the contents of *The Student Evaluation Standards*, heighten awareness of the importance and relevance of standards for student evaluation, engage participants in applying particular standards, and have them gain familiarity with the contents of *The Student Evaluation Standards*.

Activity 2.1: Overview of *The Student Evaluation Standards*

Time: 20 minutes

Objective: To introduce participants to *The Student Evaluation Standards*.

Advance Preparation: Prepare overheads of the Propriety, Utility, Feasibility, and Accuracy Standards Summaries (Appendices D1-D4).

1. Present each Standard Summary and list of standards for each category. Note the key aspects of each category—suggested comments are below.

   Propriety Standards:
   - *These standards are presented first, indicating that student welfare should be of utmost concern in any student evaluation situation. The Propriety Standards address such issues as serving student learning, student-parent rights, privacy, and access to information.*

   Utility Standards:
   - *Student evaluations should be designed to serve student learning. Evaluators should help those who use student evaluation results make the best possible use of this information to benefit students.*

   Feasibility Standards:
   - *Since student evaluations take place in the real world, evaluators need to consider the many environmental factors that can affect the quality of evaluations, such as political factors and time and other resource constraints.*

   Accuracy Standards:
   - *It is essential that student evaluations produce accurate information and that this information is interpreted correctly. Given the array of important decisions that are made based on student evaluation results, accuracy is critical.*

2. Refer participants to the tear-out sheet at the back of the Standards book for a list of all the standards statements.

Activity 2.2: The Importance and Relevance of Standards for Student Evaluation—A Case in Point

Time: 30 minutes

Objective: To introduce participants to some of the types of issues that the Student Evaluation Standards address and orient them to the need for standards.

Advance Preparation: Make copies of Case Example 1: Plagiarism Controversy (Appendix E). Familiarize yourself with the case. Prepare an overhead of Case Example 1 questions (Appendix F).

Activity:

1. Distribute copies of Case Example 1.

2. Divide participants into small groups.

3. Display the overhead of Case Example 1 questions (Appendix F):
    * *How did the events and decisions described in the case impact student learning?*
    * *What are the positive and/or negative consequences of the events described in the case?*
    * *Could this happen at your school? What is in place in your school that might prevent this from happening?*

4. Instruct participants to discuss the questions within their groups. Within 15 minutes they should agree to and write down their answers (they can use the back of the Case Example 1 handout for recording their answers).

5. Ask each group to select a spokesperson to report on the group's answers. This case may cause some heated discussion about what should or shouldn't have been done or who was at fault. Steer participants away from these issues and back to the questions presented. Let participants know that their next task will be to analyze this case using the Standards. Some key points that should be drawn out include the following:

    Impact on student learning:
    * This assignment does not appear to be well aligned with student learning expectations for biology.
    * It does not appear that students received ongoing support/guidance while completing the assignment, which was worth 50 percent of their grades. Checks on progress might have revealed that some students were not making progress on their assignments, were not gaining the desired conceptual understanding, and/or did not understand what constituted plagiarism.
    * It is likely that the students who plagiarized learned very little by completing the assignment.

Negative consequences:
- Students who did well on the assignment and did not plagiarize were penalized when the weight of the assignment was reduced from 50 percent to 30 percent.
- Because the board handled the matter behind closed doors, students, parents, and teachers did not know on what basis the decisions were made—making them appear arbitrary and politically expedient.

Positive consequences:
- The situation *might* have led to a reassessment of current student evaluation policies.
- The situation *might* have led to a reassessment of the value of the 10-year-old biology assignment against current learning objectives (such as state standards).
- The situation *might* have served as an impetus for a realignment of evaluation and instruction for the full biology course and other courses throughout the school.

Could it happen "here"?
- These factors should be considered:
  o the degree to which different parties have input into evaluation policies
  o how frequently assignments/evaluations are examined/updated
  o how susceptible teachers and board members are to political influence
  o how carefully teachers align instruction objectives and evaluation practices
  o whether the school has established guidelines and procedures for resolving disputes between teachers and students (or parents/guardians)

6. After all the groups report their answers, summarize the main themes. Encourage questions/comments among the groups.

Activity 2.3: Applying the Standards

Time: 1 hour, 15 minutes

Objective: To engage participants in applying the Standards to two cases in order to facilitate discussion about the Standards and the issues they address.

Advance Preparation: Make copies of the Standard Application Worksheet (Appendix G) and Case Example 2 (Appendix H). Participants will already have a copy of Case Example 1 (Appendix E) from the previous activity.

Activity 2.3.1: Application of the Standards to Case Example 1: Plagiarism Controversy (30 minutes)

1. Divide participants into small groups.

2. Assign one of the following standards to each group: P2, U1, F2, A10 (these standards were selected for their relevance to the case and to showcase the four major standards categories; other standards may be used, too).

3. Distribute one Standard Application Worksheet to each group.

4. Instruct participants on how to apply their assigned Standard to the case:

    - *In the* Standards *book, read about the standard you are going to apply, including the standard statement, overview, guidelines, and common errors.*
    - *Read Case Example 1.*
    - *In your small groups, search the case to identify how it met and/or failed to meet your assigned standard (referring especially to the guidelines and common errors).*
    - *Record this information on the Standard Application Worksheet.*
    - *After 15 minutes, each group will report its findings for its assigned standard. When reporting, indicate the standard you applied and read the standard statement. You will have 5 minutes to report on your standard.*

5. After the 15-minute discussion period, ask a spokesperson for each group to report the group's answers. Assign a timekeeper to make sure reporting time is limited to five minutes per standard—to ensure that each group has time to talk.

    Record each group's findings, as well as any other pertinent points offered by other participants, on a separate piece of flip chart paper. Encourage questions and discussion among the groups.

    Check the responses against the points below—which are derived from the Standards' guidelines and common errors—to make sure all the relevant points are addressed. Participants may also identify other legitimate points.

Standard P2: Appropriate Policies and Procedures	
How the case met the standard	**How the case failed to meet the standard**
• Students and parents were made aware of the definition of plagiarism and its penalty at the beginning of the semester (Guidelines B and H). • Ms. Pelton's policy concerning plagiarism was consistent with the policy for cheating stated in the student handbook (Guideline E). • Ms. Pelton followed through on her stated policy regarding plagiarism (Guideline F).	• The board's policy decision was made behind closed doors (Guideline A). • The board's decision violated school policy on student cheating (Guideline F). • The board applied policy retroactively (made up new rules to fit the situation) (Common Error C).
Standard U1: Constructive Orientation	
How the case met the standard	**How the case failed to meet the standard**
• None noted	• It is likely that parents, students, and administrators did not completely understand the evaluation's purpose and expectations or how it would serve student learning (Guideline A; Common Error C). • Ms. Pelton did not provide any evaluative feedback on this very important assignment until it was completed (Guideline B). • Ms. Pelton took a "gotcha" approach to the evaluation (Guideline C).

Standard F2: Political Viability	
How the case met the standard	**How the case failed to meet the standard**
• Ms. Pelton asked parents and students to read and sign her class syllabus at the beginning of the semester (Guideline A; Common Error A). • The dispute was handled swiftly (if not effectively) (Guideline E).	• The board did not follow its established policies concerning student cheating (Guideline A). • The leaf project was a decade old. It is likely that few of the parties involved in this case were involved in developing the leaf project and assigning its worth of 50 percent of the semester grade (Guidelines B and F; Common Error C). • The closed-session decision to change the penalty for plagiarism undermined the established policy and the credibility of Ms. Pelton (Guideline D). • Parent and board feedback on the assignment and evaluation was received in a reactive rather than proactive manner (Guideline F; Common Error C).
Standard A10: Justified Conclusions	
How the case met the standard	**How the case failed to meet the standard**
• Ms. Pelton's decision to give the plagiarizing students a zero for their projects was justified, given her stated policy (Guideline A). • Ms. Pelton's policy regarding student cheating was consistent with the schoolwide policy (Guideline B).	• It is not clear that Ms. Pelton provided students and parents with a scoring guide or rubric for how she would evaluate the assignment (Guideline E). • The board used its authority to change the project's weight and reduce the plagiarism penalty, without providing justification for doing so (Common Error C).

Activity 2.3.2: Application of the Standards to Case Example 2—Math Learning Communities (30 minutes)

1. Distribute copies of Case Example 2—Math Learning Communities.

2. Participants may continue in the same small groups, or you may create new groups.

3. Assign one of the following standards to each group: P1, U4, F1, A9 (these standards were selected for their relevance to the case and to showcase the four major standards categories; other standards may be used, too).

4. Distribute a new set of Standard Application Worksheets (one per group).

5. Instruct participants to follow the same process they used with the first case example.

6. After the 15-minute discussion period, ask a spokesperson for each group to report the group's answers. Assign a timekeeper to make sure reporting time is limited to 5 minutes per standard—to ensure that each group has time to report.

    Record each group's findings, as well as any other pertinent points offered by other participants, on a separate piece of flip chart paper. Encourage questions and discussion among the groups.

    Check the responses against the points below—which are derived from the Standards' guidelines and common errors—to make sure all the relevant points are addressed. Participants may also identify other legitimate points.

Standard P1: Service to Students	
How the case met the standard	**How the case failed to meet the standard**
• Assessments are keyed to learning objectives (Guidelines A and D). • Individual students are regularly provided with feedback on their personal progress (Guideline C). • Students are involved in the evaluation process (through self-assessments) and can chart their learning (Guideline E). • At the schools where assessments are sent home weekly, parents can see how the evaluation supports learning and how their children are progressing (Guidelines F and H). • Assessments are provided in both Spanish and English (Guideline G). • The need for more uniform and useful reporting to parents and guardians has been recognized and plans to address this are being developed (Guideline H). • Students are given frequent, regular opportunities to demonstrate their knowledge/skills (Common Error A). • The program serves school accountability as well as individual student learning. (Common Errors B and D).	• Report cards alone may not provide parents/guardians with useful and understandable information about their children's progress (Guideline H).

Standard U4: Evaluator Qualifications	
How the case met the standard	**How the case failed to meet the standard**
<ul><li>The program serves student learning while also providing teachers with an opportunity to reflect on and improve how their teaching and assessment strategies impact student learning (Guideline A).</li><li>The program models sound evaluation practices and use and handling of evaluation information (Guideline B).</li><li>It is likely that district personnel carefully developed and reviewed the program before implemented it at the participating schools (Guideline C).</li></ul>	<ul><li>Because of the need to use standardized assessments in this program, it is not clear that the teachers were given any guidance for developing their own assessments or using alternative assessment techniques (although other professional development activities in the schools may address this, if it is a need) (Guideline E).</li></ul>

Standard F1: Practical Orientation	
How the case met the standard	**How the case failed to meet the standard**
<ul><li>Assessments are keyed to learning objectives (Guideline A).</li><li>Assessments are provided in both Spanish and English (Guideline F).</li><li>Students' confidentiality is protected through aggregation of scores (Guideline H).</li></ul>	<ul><li>It is not clear that alternative assessment procedures are available for students with learning disabilities (Guideline F).</li></ul>

Standard A9: Analysis of Information	
How the case met the standard	**How the case failed to meet the standard**
<ul><li>Weekly analysis of aggregated and individual assessment results supports the purpose of tracking and enhancing individual student learning and efficacy of teaching strategies (Guideline A).</li><li>Assessments are keyed to state-mandated learning objectives (Guideline B).</li><li>It is likely that the district validated the assessments and scoring procedure before implementing the program (Guideline C).</li><li>Item analysis is used regularly to provide insights about the students' understanding in relation to learning objectives (Guideline P).</li><li>Quantitative analysis enables the assessments to be scored and analyzed in a timely manner to support weekly review of progress in learning and teaching (Common Error A)</li></ul>	<ul><li>It is not clear if students and parents/guardians are provided with any written comments or visual displays in reports on student progress (Guidelines E, N, and O).</li></ul>

Activity 2.3.2: Case Examples Discussion (15 minutes)

1. Ask participants to reflect on the two case examples and discuss the questions as a group (collectively—not within small groups):
   - *How did information contained in the Standards affect your thinking about the cases (did it change your mind about either of the cases, confirm your feelings, and/or raise issues about the cases you hadn't thought of)?*
   - *How would advance use of the Standards by the parties involved have affected either of the cases?*

Activity 2.4: Standards Treasure Hunt

Time: 20 minutes

Objective: To have participants gain familiarity with the organization and content of the Standards by looking for certain pieces of information.

Advance Preparation: Photocopy and cut up the Treasure Hunt Questions (Appendix I) so that each question is on a separate slip of paper. Fold the slips and mix them up in a container from which participant groups will draw questions.

Activity:

1. Divide participants into small groups.

2. Pass the container of treasure hunt questions around, asking each group to draw a certain number of questions (e.g., 5 to 8 questions, depending on how many small groups there are).

3. Instruct participants to work within their groups to find the answers to the questions, record their answers (and any comments/questions about the information) on the slips of paper, along with where they found the information. They may also use sticky notes to record individual comments/questions and mark pages in the book.

4. After 10 minutes, select questions (from the list below) and have members of the group that had that question read their answers and indicate where they found the answer (i.e., the section or standard in which the information was located). If they have any comments or questions about the information they found, they should share those as well.

   You do not need to go through all the questions, but have each group report on at least 2 or 3 questions. Answers to the questions are as follows:

Question	Answer	Location
1. Where can you find a list of standards that are especially relevant to developing student evaluation policy?	Functional Table of Contents	p. ix
2. Where can you find a list of standards that are especially relevant to evaluating students from diverse backgrounds?	Functional Table of Contents	p. xi
3. Where can you find a list of standards that are especially relevant to ensuring fairness?	Functional Table of Contents	p. x

Question	Answer	Location
4. Where can you find a list of standards that are especially relevant to communicating and reporting student evaluation information?	Functional Table of Contents	p. viii
5. The Joint Committee recommends five steps in applying the standards. What are they?	1. Become very familiar with the standards 2. Clarify your purpose(s) for applying the standards 3. Review and select one or more appropriate standards 4. Apply the standards that you have selected 5. Based on your application of the standards, decide on and implement a course of action	p. 11
6. What are the possible ratings for whether something met the standards? (See "Resource B")?	• met • partially met • not met • not applicable	p. 221
7. The Student Evaluation Standards are approved by ANSI. What does ANSI stand for?	American National Standards Institute	back cover and other places
8. What is Corwin Press's logo and motto?	• logo: raven on an open book • motto: Success for All Learners	p. xxiv
9. What section of the Standards book is *not* copyrighted?	• the tear-out standards summary	last page of the book
10. What is the Web site address for the Joint Committee on Standards for Educational Evaluation?	• http://jc.wmich.edu/	p. xviii
11. What is a major threat to evaluation being of service to students? (See caveats for Standard P1—Service to Students)	• the press for accountability	p. 29

Question	Answer	Location
12. Name five issues that should be addressed in written student evaluation policies. (See explanation for Standard P2—Appropriate Policies and Procedures)	• equity and fairness in matters of race and sex • allowable alternatives for students with special needs and/or limited language competence • student cheating and plagiarism • grading and reporting procedures • how excused and unexcused absences are treated • student grievance and appeal procedures • confidentiality of student evaluation information • skills and qualifications of evaluators	p. 33
13. Is it acceptable to publicly announce favorable information about a student? Under what conditions? (See guidelines and common errors for Standard P3—Access to Information)	Yes, but only if prior consent is obtained (Common Error A)	p. 41
14. What information about an evaluation process should be provided to students and parents/guardians? (See guidelines and common errors for Standard P4—Treatment of Students)	• assessment methods/procedures • how the information will be used • appeal process (Guideline A)	p. 46
15. Student rights are grounded based on what factors? (See explanation for Standard P5)	• law • school policy • ethical practice • common sense • courtesy	p. 51
16. What are the typical frames of reference for identifying the strengths and weaknesses of a student's performance? (See explanation for Standard P6—Balanced Evaluation)	• relation to specified standards • relation to peers • relation to aptitude or expected growth • amount of improvement • amount learned	p. 55
17. What should a teacher do if he or she cannot eliminate the potential for a conflict of interest? (See guidelines and common errors for Standard P7—Conflict of Interest)	Define the procedures to be followed in writing (Guideline C)	p. 60

Question	Answer	Location
18. What should a constructive student evaluation result in? (See standard statement for U1—Constructive Orientation)	• educational decisions that are in the best interest of the student	p. 67
19. Is it generally safe to assume that most audiences for student evaluation information have the same or similar needs? (See guidelines and common errors for Standard U2 Defined Users and Uses)	No (Common Error A)	p. 72
20. If the scope of information collected for a student evaluation is too narrow or too broad, what are the possible consequences? (See rationale for Standard U3—Information Scope)	• too narrow: there will be insufficient information to make meaningful decisions • too broad: instructional time will be wasted collecting inappropriate or irrelevant information	p. 77
21. What qualifications should a person who evaluates students have? (See explanation for Standard U4—Evaluator Qualifications)	The ability to • create or select appropriate assessments • collect data and information accurately • interpret data and information accurately • make and communicate sound decisions	p. 83
22. What are the common errors associated with Standard U5—Explicit Values?	• failing to recognize alternative sources of values • imposing a set of inappropriate values • using evaluation criteria or procedures that are inconsistent with the prescribed values of the state, school district, and/or school	p. 91
23. The extent to which evaluation reports are influential and useful depends on what factors? (See explanation for Standard U6—Effective Reporting)	• clarity • timeliness • accuracy • relevance	p. 95
24. What is a possible negative side effect of follow-up activities to improve performance in a certain area? (See guidelines and common errors for Standard U6—Follow-Up)	• concentrating on one subject to the detriment of others	p. 102

Question	Answer	Location
25. Educators should always seek out assessment shortcuts to economize resources: True or false? (See guidelines and common errors for Standard F1)	False (Common Error C)	p. 109
26. From whom should feedback on student evaluations be obtained? (See guidelines and common errors for Standard F2—Political Viability)	<ul><li>students</li><li>parents/guardians</li><li>teachers</li><li>administrators</li><li>other appropriate users</li></ul>	p. 114
27. When determining the costs of an evaluation, it is a common error to fail to include costs for what tasks? (See common errors for Standard F3—Evaluation Support)	<ul><li>assistance in analyzing the quality of instruments</li><li>interpreting external standardized test results</li></ul>	p. 121
28. Standard A1 is Validity Orientation. What is the definition of validity?	<ul><li>the degree to which inferences drawn from the results of the assessment method(s) about the knowledge, skills, attitudes, and behaviors demonstrated by each student are trustworthy and appropriate for making decisions about students</li></ul>	pp. 127 & 232
29. A sound evaluation requires that one first specify what expectations? (See rationale for Standard A2—Defined Expectations for Students)	<ul><li>what the student is to learn</li><li>the qualifications a student should bring to the learning situation</li><li>how the student is to act and respond in learning and evaluation situations</li></ul>	p. 138
30. What are some student-level contextual factors that can influence student learning? (See explanation for Standard A3—Context Analysis).	<ul><li>prior knowledge</li><li>completion of school homework</li><li>language capability</li><li>home learning environment</li><li>learning and physical disabilities</li></ul>	p. 143
31. Both low-stakes and high-stakes evaluations should be equally well documented: True or false? (See caveats for Standard U4—Documented Procedures)	False	p. 150
32. What are two things teachers must weigh against the need for appropriate and defensible student evaluation information? (See caveats for Standard U5—Defensible Information)	<ul><li>expedience</li><li>convenience</li></ul>	p. 157

Question	Answer	Location
33. Standard A6 is Reliable Information. What is the definition of reliability?	• the degree of consistency of the scores or information obtained from an information-gathering process. • a measure of how consistent the results obtained in an assessment are in a norm-referenced evaluation situation; consistency of a student's ranking within the group of students against which the student is being compared	pp. 161 & 231
34. What are some of the bias-related variables that might affect the collection and interpretation of information in a student evaluation? (See explanation for Standard A7—Bias Identification and Management)	• cultural differences • language differences • physical, mental, and developmental disabilities • athletic or aesthetic prowess • political connections • gender or racial stereotyping • socioeconomic status	p. 167
35. It is generally safe to assume that machine/computer-scored tests are accurate: True or false? (See guidelines and common errors for Standard A8—Handling Information and Quality Control)	False (Common Error A)	p. 176
36. When teachers have a choice, they should use quantitative methods rather than qualitative methods for analyzing student evaluation information: True or false? (See caveats for Standard A9—Analysis of Information)	False	p. 184
37. What information should be included in a written student evaluation framework? (See guidelines and common errors for Standard A10—Justified Conclusions)	• student learning objectives • content breakdowns • needed performance information • sources of evidence • guides for analyzing data and information • guides for making interpretations and drawing conclusions	p. 198
38. Standard A11 is Metaevaluation. What is the definition of metaevaluation?	• an evaluation of an evaluation	pp. 203 & 230

3. Conclusion

The activities presented in this section are intended to facilitate reflection of the information presented, have participants identify how they will use the Standards, review workshop objectives and expectations and tie up any loose ends, and get feedback on the workshop.

Activity 3.1: Pair-Share Discussion

Time: 20 minutes

Objective: To have participants reflect on the material presented and identify how they will use the Standards.

Advance Preparation: Make copies of the Pair-Share Questions (Appendix J).

Activity:

1. Divide participants into pairs.

2. Distribute copies of the Pair-Share Questions.

3. Instruct participants to interview their partners and record their partners' answers to the following questions:
   - *What policies, practices, issues in your classroom, school, district, etc., would benefit from a review against* The Student Evaluation Standards*?*
   - *How will you apply what you've learned about the Standards? Give at least two or three examples, indicating what you will do, why, and when.*

4. After about 10 minutes, ask each person to share something his or her partner said in response to the questions.

5. Encourage questions/comments from the rest of the group.

Activity 3.2: Review

Time: 10 minutes

Objective: To review workshop objectives and expectations identified at the start of the workshop, summarize important concepts, and address any lingering questions/issues.

Advance Preparation: Make sure the recorded workshop objectives and expectations are visible.

Activity:

1. Review the preset workshop objectives and other expectations voiced by participants at the beginning of the workshop—if they are still posted in the room, direct participants' attention to them.

2. Ask participants if each objective/expectation was covered in sufficient depth. If not, ask participants to suggest how further learning could take place (e.g., additional workshops, study groups, etc.).

3. Ask for additional comments/questions. If you do not have the answer to a question or there is not sufficient time for a complete answer, discuss with the participants options for obtaining additional information.

Activity 3.3: Workshop Evaluation

Time: 10 minutes

Objective: To obtain evaluative feedback on the effectiveness and relevance of the workshop.

Advance Preparation: Make copies of the Workshop Evaluation Form (Appendix K), or create your own.

Activity:

1. Distribute copies of the Workshop Evaluation Form.

2. Ask participants to complete the form; they should not put their names on the forms.

3. Collect the forms.

4. At a later time, review the evaluations and use the information to modify future workshops.

Resources

Evaluation Standards

American Educational Research Association, American Psychological Association, & National Council on Measurement. (1999). *Standards for educational and psychological testing.* Washington, DC: American Educational Research Association.

American Federation of Teachers, National Council on Measurement, & National Education Association. (1990). *Standards for teacher competence in educational assessment of students.* Washington, DC: National Council on Measurement in Education.

Joint Advisory Committee. (1993). *Principles for fair student assessment practices for education in Canada.* Edmonton, Alberta, Canada: University of Alberta, Centre for Research in Applied Measurement and Evaluation.

Joint Committee on Standards for Educational Evaluation, Daniel L. Stufflebeam, Chair. (1988). *The personnel evaluation standards.* Thousand Oaks, CA: Corwin.

Joint Committee on Standards for Educational Evaluation, James R. Sanders, Chair. (1994). *The program evaluation standards* (2nd ed.). Thousand Oaks, CA: Sage.

Joint Committee on Standards for Educational Evaluation, Arlen R. Gullickson, Chair. (2003). *The student evaluation standards.* Thousand Oaks, CA: A joint publication of Corwin Press and the ETS Educational Policy Leadership Institute.

Joint Committee on Standards for Educational Evaluation. http://www.wmich.edu/evalctr/jc/

Professional Development, Training, and Facilitation

American Society for Training and Development. http://www.astd.org

Bens, I. (1999). *Facilitation at a glance.* Salem, NH: AQP/Participative Dynamics/GOAL/QPC. http://www.goalqpc.com

3M Meeting Network. *Be a competent facilitator.* http://www.3m.com/meetingnetwork/readingroom/facilitation.html

Hassel, E. *Professional development: Learning from the best: A toolkit for schools and districts based on the National Awards Program for Model Professional Development.* Naperville, IL: North Central Regional Educational Laboratory. http://www.ncrel.org/pd/toolkit.htm

National Staff Development Council. http://www.nsdc.org

Student Assessment and Evaluation

Airasian, P. (2000). *Classroom assessment: Concepts and applications* (4th ed.). Boston: McGraw-Hill.

Black, P., & Wiliam, D. (1998). Inside the black box: Raising standards through classroom assessment. *Phi Delta Kappan, 80*(2): 139–144, 146–148. http://www.pdkmembers.org/

Committee on the Foundations of Assessment, Pelligrino, J., Chudowsky, N., and Glaser, R., (Eds.). (2001). *Knowing what students know: The science and design of educational assessments.* Washington, DC: National Academy Press. http://www.nap.edu/

Lin, R. L., & Gronlund, N. E. (2000). *Measurement and assessment in teaching* (8th ed.). Upper Saddle River, NJ: Prentice Hall.

Oosterhof, A. (1990). *Classroom applications of educational measurement.* Columbus, OH: Merrill.

Practical Assessment, Research, and Evaluation (Online journal). College Park, MD: Department of Measurement, Statistics, and Evaluation, University of Maryland, http://ericae.net/pare/

Stiggins, R. J. (2001). *Student-involved classroom assessment* (3rd ed.). Upper Saddle River, NJ: Prentice-Hall, Inc.

Workshop Materials

Appendix A

Sample Letter to Accompany Standards Book

[date]

[recipient's name]
[recipient's address]

Dear _____:

Thank you for signing up for the Student Evaluation Standards workshop on [date].

To ensure that the workshop is as productive and beneficial as possible, please review the enclosed copy of *The Student Evaluation Standards*. At a minimum, please read the book's introduction and the complete information for at least one standard.

Please be sure to bring your copy of *The Student Evaluation Standards* with you to the workshop. This is very important, since we will be using the book for several activities.

Sincerely,

[workshop organizer]

enc

Appendix B

Student Evaluation Standards Workshop
Sample Agenda

Objectives:
- develop a common understanding of the nature of student evaluation, including the range of activities and purposes associated with student evaluation
- become acquainted with the contents and organization of *The Student Evaluation Standards*
- apply the Standards in order to understand their relevance and applicability
- identify ways to use the Standards

Schedule:

8:30-8:50	Introductions
8:50-9:20	Student Evaluation Perceptions & Expectations
9:20-9:35	Workshop Objectives and Expectations
9:35-10:20	The Nature of Student Evaluation
10:20-10:35	Break
10:35-10:55	Overview of the Standards
10:55-11:25	The Importance and Relevance of the Student Evaluation Standards
11:25-11:55	Applying the Standards (Case 1)
11:55-1:00	Lunch
1:00-1:45	Applying the Standards (Case 2 & Discussion)
1:45-2:05	Treasure Hunt
2:05-2:25	Pair-Share
2:25-2:40	Review
2:40-2:50	Workshop Evaluation

Appendix C

Definition of Student Evaluation

The process of systematically collecting and interpreting information that can be used (1) to inform students and their parents/guardians about the progress they are making toward attaining the knowledge, skills, attitudes, and behaviors to be learned or acquired; and (2) to inform the various personnel who make educational decisions (instructional, diagnostic, placement, promotion, graduation) about students.

Appendix D-1

Propriety Standards Summary

Propriety Standards help ensure that student evaluations will be conducted legally, ethically, and with due regard for the well-being of the students being evaluated as well as other people affected by the evaluation results.

P1 Service to Students

P2 Appropriate Policies and Procedures

P3 Access to Evaluation Information

P4 Treatment of Students

P5 Rights of Students

P6 Balanced Evaluation

P7 Conflict of Interest

Appendix D-2

Utility Standards Summary

Utility Standards help ensure that student evaluations are useful. Useful student evaluations are informative, timely, and influential.

U1 Constructive Orientation

U2 Defined Users and Uses

U3 Information Scope

U4 Evaluation Qualifications

U5 Explicit Values

U6 Effective Reporting

U7 Follow-Up

Appendix D-3

Feasibility Standards Summary

Feasibility Standards help ensure that student evaluations can be implemented as planned. Feasible evaluations are practical, diplomatic, and adequately supported.

F1 Practical Orientation

F2 Political Viability

F3 Evaluation Support

Appendix D-4

Accuracy Standards Summary

Accuracy Standards help ensure that a student evaluation will produce sound information about a student's learning and performance. Sound information leads to valid interpretations, justifiable conclusions, and appropriate follow-up.

A1 Validity Orientation

A2 Defined Expectations for Students

A3 Context Analysis

A4 Documented Procedures

A5 Defensible Information

A6 Reliable Information

A7 Bias Identification and Management

A8 Handling Information and Quality Control

A9 Analysis of Information

A10 Justified Conclusions

A11 Metaevaluation

Appendix E

Case Example 1: Plagiarism Controversy

The trouble began last fall when Ms. Pelton, a second-year biology teacher, concluded that 28 of her 118 students had plagiarized portions of a major project and gave them grades of zero for it.

A crowd of parents brought complaints to the Dec. 11 meeting of the Piper school board. They questioned the severity of the penalty and asked whether students had been instructed in the nuances of plagiarism. Some later suggested that Ms. Pelton's inexperience in the classroom had played a role. Other parents, however, have backed the teacher.

In fact, the teacher had asked parents and students to read and sign a class syllabus in September that laid out the definition of plagiarism and the penalty—similar to the penalty for cheating described in the school's student handbook.

The project, on leaves, had been a fixture of the sophomore year at Piper High for the past decade. Rising sophomores, starting in summer, collected leaves from the school grounds and their neighborhoods, measured and described them and the trees they came from, and by December each produced a report that would be worth 50 percent of his or her semester grade.

Ms. Pelton said she confirmed that students had cribbed leaf descriptions when she "checked out all the [botany] books in the library," and submitted papers to a commercial online database designed to catch plagiarists. Mr. Adams, the principal, also checked some projects after receiving the first parental complaints, and he agreed there was plagiarism.

The incident grew into a tempest only after the Dec. 11 board meeting—and district Superintendent Michael Rooney's emergence from a closed session with the board to say the students' penalty would be reduced. The next day, Mr. Rooney directed Ms. Pelton to change the project's weight from 50 percent to 30 percent of the course's semester grade. And he said that 600 points should be taken from the plagiarists, rather than the entire 1,800 points the project was worth.

Ms. Pelton resigned in protest the same day.

"I'd lost the kids' respect. I heard kids talking about that if they didn't like what I did in the future, they could go to the board of education and they could change that," she said in an interview last week.

Ms. Pelton said that she felt undercut by the school board, and she contended that the decision also was unfair to students who had completed their projects without cheating. The grading change allowed 27 of the 28 students to escape an F, but it also pulled down the grades for about 20 students who had not plagiarized.

Board members, in turn, said last week they felt pressured to resolve a dispute that school administrators should have handled.

Source: As first appeared in *Education Week*, April 3, 2002. Reprinted with permission. The complete article is available from http://www.edweek.org/

Appendix F

Case Example 1 Questions

1. How did the events and decisions described in the case impact student learning?

2. What are the positive and/or negative consequences of the events described in the case?

3. Could this happen in your school? What is in place in your school that might prevent this from happening?

Appendix G

Standard Application Worksheet

Name of Standard: _____

How did the case meet the standard?	How did the case fail to meet the standard?

Appendix H

Case Example 2: Math Learning Community

Like school districts across the United States, Dallas Independent School District (DISD) is facing increasing pressure for improved student achievement. DISD is a large urban district made up mostly of minority students from low-income families. Students' math scores on the state-mandated achievement tests have been below the state average for several years. To address the issue, the district is piloting "Math Learning Communities" in several elementary schools. The program targets math teaching in grades 2 through 6 and is now being implemented in about 40 schools.

Each student is given a Learning Target Chart* that identifies the concepts that will be covered in a 6-week math unit. As the students are introduced to new topics and gain proficiency in them, they mark the appropriate cells in the chart, progressing from "I've heard of this" to "I can do this with some help" to "I can do this on my own" and finally, "I can teach someone else." It is the students' responsibility to track their learning. It is a self-assessment tool, and the teacher does not check the charts.

Each week, the students complete an assessment of 12 to 16 items on 3 or 4 state-mandated math objectives (the concepts covered in the 6-week unit). Each assessment covers a basic skills objective, a word-problem objective, and a higher order objective. The assessments are provided in both English and Spanish. The assessment results are submitted to the school's central office. Teachers receive an aggregated report for their entire class, plus results for individual students.

The results are also aggregated by grade level. This information serves as the basis for teacher discussion. Teachers in a participating school meet weekly in 45-minute sessions to analyze the weekly assessment results, discuss math concepts and teaching strategies, and track student progress. They identify what concepts students are having trouble with and discuss possible causes. Based on their discussion, teachers adapt their teaching strategies.

At some of the participating schools, the assessments are sent home weekly. Students correct any items they missed, parents sign them, and the students turn them in to their teachers as homework. Other reporting mechanisms, such as individualized, 6-week progress reports for parents and/or student-led parent-teacher conferences, are being considered at some schools. All students in the district receive report cards every six weeks.

Source: Based on Bearden, D. (2002). *Data as a motivating factor for improvement: Raising achievement through math learning communities.* Paper presented at the annual meeting of the Consortium for Research on Educational Accountability and Teacher Evaluation, Boise, ID.

* The Learning Target Chart is based on the Capacity Matrix tool developed by David Langford, Langford International, Inc.

Appendix I

Treasure Hunt Questions

Question	Answer	Location
1. Where can you find a list of standards that are especially relevant to developing student evaluation policy?		

Question	Answer	Location
2. Where can you find a list of standards that are especially relevant to evaluating students from diverse backgrounds?		

Question	Answer	Location
3. Where can you find a list of standards that are especially relevant to ensuring fairness?		

Question	Answer	Location
4. Where can you find a list of standards that are especially relevant to communicating and reporting student evaluation information?		

Question	Answer	Location
5. The Joint Committee recommends five steps in applying the standards. What are they?		

Question	Answer	Location
6. What are the possible ratings for whether something met the standards? (See Resource B)		

Question	Answer	Location
7. The Student Evaluation Standards are approved by ANSI. What does ANSI stand for?		

Question	Answer	Location
8. What is Corwin Press's logo and motto?		

Question	Answer	Location
9. What section of the Standards book is *not* copyrighted?		

Question	Answer	Location
10. What is the Web site address for the Joint Committee on Standards for Educational Evaluation?		

Question	Answer	Location
11. What is a major threat to evaluation being of service to students? (See caveats for Standard P1—Service to Students)		

Question	Answer	Location
12. Name five issues that should be addressed in written student evaluation policies. (See explanation for Standard P2— Appropriate Policies and Procedures)		

Question	Answer	Location
13. Is it acceptable to publicly announce favorable information about a student? Under what conditions? (See guidelines and common errors for Standard P3—Access to Information)		

Question	Answer	Location
14. What information about an evaluation process should be provided to students and parents/guardians? (See guidelines and common errors for Standard P4—Treatment of Students)		

Question	Answer	Location
15. Student rights are grounded based on what factors? (See explanation for Standard P5)		

Question	Answer	Location
16. What are the typical frames of reference for identifying the strengths and weaknesses of a students' performance? (See explanation for Standard P6—Balanced Evaluation)		

Question	Answer	Location
17. What should a teacher do if he or she cannot eliminate the potential for a conflict of interest? (See guidelines and common errors for Standard P7—Conflict of Interest)		

Question	Answer	Location
18. What should constructive student evaluation result in? (See standard statement for U1—Constructive Orientation)		

Question	Answer	Location
19. Is it generally safe to assume that most audiences for student evaluation information have the same or similar needs? (See guidelines and common errors for Standard U2 Defined Users and Uses)		

Question	Answer	Location
20. If the scope of information collected for a student evaluation is too narrow or too broad, what are the possible consequences? (See rationale for Standard U3— Information Scope)		

Question	Answer	Location
21. What qualifications should a person who evaluates students have? (See explanation for Standard U4—Evaluator Qualifications)		

Question	Answer	Location
22. What are the common errors associated with Standard U5—Explicit Values?		

Question	Answer	Location
23. The extent to which evaluation reports are influential and useful depends on what factors? (See explanation for Standard U6—Effective Reporting)		

Question	Answer	Location
24. What is a possible negative side effect of follow-up activities to improve performance in a certain area? (See guidelines and common errors for Standard U6—Follow-Up)		

Question	Answer	Location
25. Educators should always seek out assessment shortcuts to economize resources: True or false? (See guidelines and common errors for Standard F1)		

Question	Answer	Location
26. From whom should feedback on student evaluations be obtained? (See guidelines and common errors for Standard F2—Political Viability)		

Question	Answer	Location
27. When determining the costs of an evaluation, it is a common error to fail to include costs for what tasks? (See common errors for Standard F3—Evaluation Support)		

Question	Answer	Location
28. Standard A1 is Validity Orientation. What is the definition of validity?		

Question	Answer	Location
29. A sound evaluation requires that one first specify what expectations? (See rationale for Standard A2—Defined Expectations for Students)		

Question	Answer	Location
30. What are some student-level contextual factors that can influence student learning? (See explanation for Standard A3—Context Analysis)		

Question	Answer	Location
31. Both low-stakes and high-stakes evaluations should be equally well documented: True or false? (See caveats for Standard U4—Documented Procedures)		

Question	Answer	Location
32. What are two things teachers must weigh against the need for appropriate and defensible student evaluation information? (See caveats for Standard U5—Defensible Information)		

Question	Answer	Location
33. Standard A6 is Reliable Information. What is the definition of reliability?		

Question	Answer	Location
34. What are some of the bias-related variables that might affect the collection and interpretation of information in a student evaluation? (See explanation for Standard A7—Bias Identification and Management)		

Question	Answer	Location
35. It is generally safe to assume that machine/computer-scored tests are accurate: True or false? (See guidelines and common errors for Standard A8—Handling Information and Quality Control)		

Question	Answer	Location
36. When teachers have a choice, they should use quantitative methods rather than qualitative methods for analyzing student evaluation information: True or false? (See caveats for Standard A9—Analysis of Information)		

Question	Answer	Location
37. What information should be included in a written student evaluation framework? (See guidelines and common errors for Standard A10—Justified Conclusions)		

Question	Answer	Location
38. Standard A11 is Metaevaluation. What is the definition of metaevaluation?		

Appendix J

Pair-Share Questions

1. What policies, practices, issues in your classroom, school, district, etc., would benefit from a review against *The Student Evaluation Standards*?

2. How will you apply what you've learned about the standards? Give at least two or three examples, indicating what you will do, why, and when:

Action: What are you going to do?	Reason: Why is it important to do?	Deadline: When are you going to do it?

Appendix K

Workshop Evaluation Form

1. What parts of the workshop were most valuable to you?

2. What parts of the workshop were least valuable to you?

3. Was there anything covered in this workshop that you are confused about or would like more information about?

	Excellent	Good	Fair	Poor
4. Presentation	❑	❑	❑	❑
5. Organization	❑	❑	❑	❑
6. Content	❑	❑	❑	❑
7. Pace	❑	❑	❑	❑

	Strongly Agree	Agree	Disagree	Strongly Disagree
8. I will use the information I learned today	❑	❑	❑	❑
9. I will recommend this workshop to others	❑	❑	❑	❑

10. Additional comments/suggestions for improvement:

**CORWIN
PRESS**

The Corwin Press logo—a raven striding across an open book—represents the happy union of courage and learning. We are a professional-level publisher of books and journals for K-12 educators, and we are committed to creating and providing resources that embody these qualities. Corwin's motto is "Success for All Learners."